by Meg Michael

illustrated by Susanne DeMarco

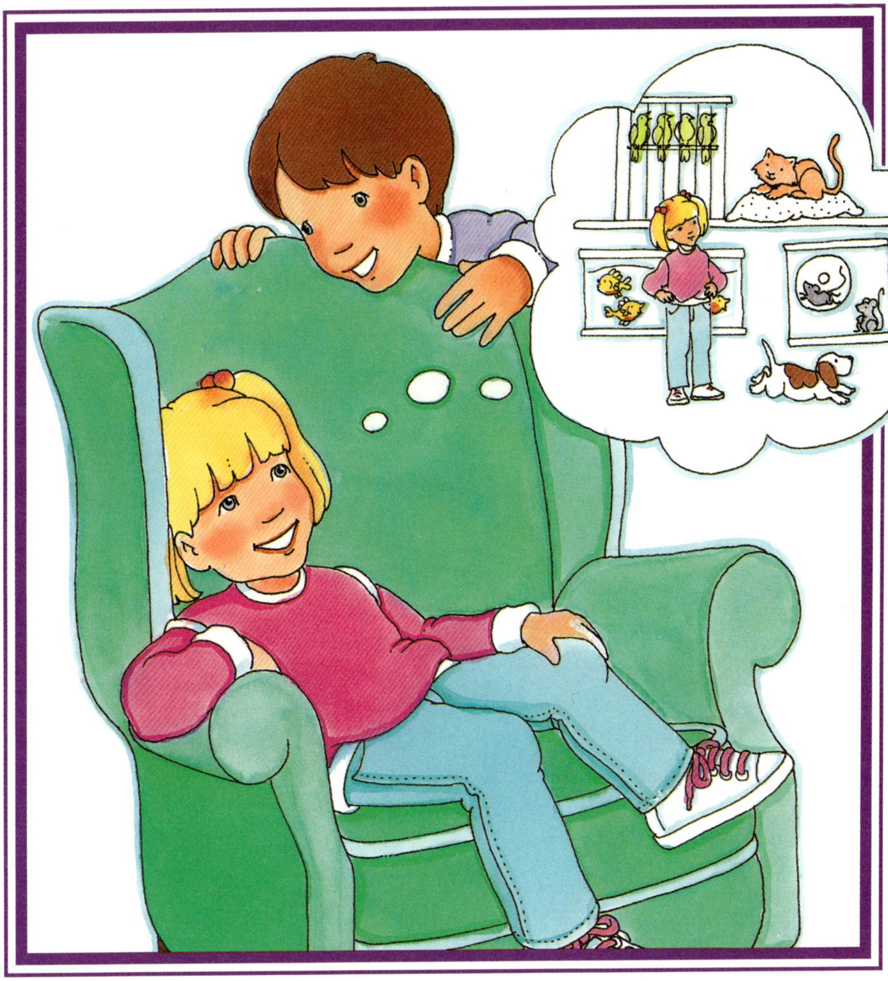

Columbus, Ohio

A Division of The ***McGraw·Hill*** *Companies*

SRA/McGraw-Hill

A Division of The ***McGraw·Hill*** *Companies*

Printed in the United States of America.

Send all inquiries to:
SRA/McGraw-Hill
250 Old Wilson Bridge Road
Suite 310
Worthington, OH 43085

ISBN 0-02-674313-2
4 5 6 7 8 9 SEG 00 99 98

: I want a pet.

: Do you want a bird?

: No, I do not want a bird.

: Then do you want a turtle?

: No, not a turtle.

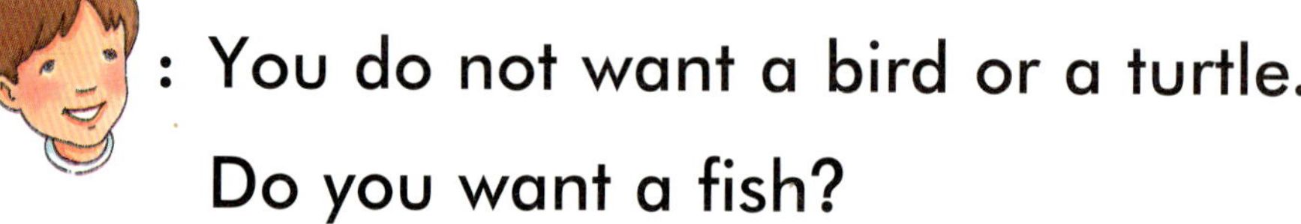

: You do not want a bird or a turtle.

Do you want a fish?

: No, I do not want a fish
or a bird or a turtle.

: I bet you want a chimp.

: No, I do not want a chimp!
I do not want a bird or a turtle
or a fish or a chimp.

: Perhaps you want a caterpillar.

A caterpillar will turn into a moth.

: No! A caterpillar will not do.
I do not want a bird or a turtle
or a fish or a chimp
or a caterpillar.

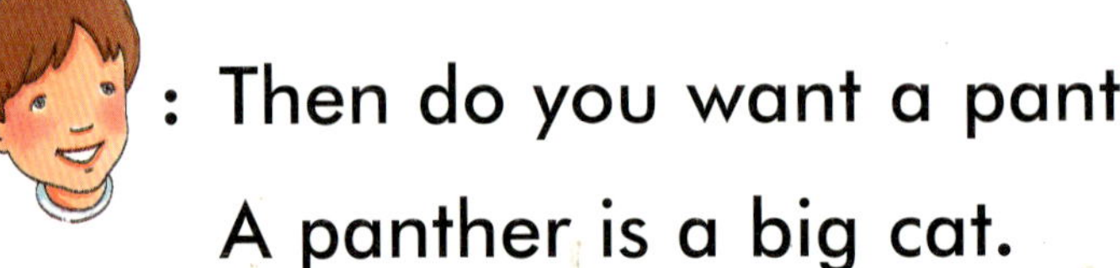

: Then do you want a panther?

A panther is a big cat.

: No! A panther is not a good pet. I do not want a bird or a turtle or a fish. I do not want a chimp or a caterpillar or a panther.

: Then what pet do you want?

: I want an octopus.

: An octopus! Then you must tell him to keep his hands off my stuff.